Flowers and Light: Poems of Life, Love, and Hope

Kendra Dartez

Kendra Dartez

Copyright © 2017 Kendra Dartez

All rights reserved.

ISBN-13: 978-1979433969

DEDICATION

This poetry book is dedicated to my mother who has always encouraged me to share my poetry with others. She truly has given me a legacy of love. I love you, Mom!

Kendra Dartez

Kendra Dartez

CONTENTS

Acknowledgments	I
Seasons	1
My Old Home	2
Only with You	4
The Thrill of the Coin	6
Stolen	8
Without You	10
A Petal	12
White Carnation	14
I Miss You	16
I Picked It	18
The Water Stirred	20
Timeless Treasure	22
The Pearl	23
Our Love is Like the Sea	24
Our Story	26
A Golden Field	28
Legacy of Love	30
My Summers with You	19
Little Old Tree	20

My Son	32
Daughter of My Heart	34
My Summers With You	36
Little Old Tree	38
Out of the Shadows	40
Sailing in the Sky	42
The Lark	43
In God We Trust	44
Autumn Has Come	46
Dare to Discover	48
A Time to Sing	50

Kendra Dartez

ACKNOWLEDGMENTS

This collection has included many of my poems written over the last twenty years. I would like to thank my parents, my husband, and all of the many teachers and friends who have encouraged my writing. I would also like to thank God for always being the light of hope when things seem dark. May these little poems bring just a little bit of hope to your heart as the writing of them did for mine!

Kendra Dartez

Seasons

Summer sun sets the soil ablaze;
It warms to the touch of the rays
As happiness shines over the sight,
The sands glow more sparkly and bright.

Then the passion dies and autumn appears.
And leaves fall to the soil in tears.
Winds of rage sweep the soil away,
Yet the sun still rises with each day.

Winter is bitter, cold, and gray;
All warm comfort fades away.
The snow drops and the evil wind takes toll
As ice freezes the soil's soul.

Beloved spring comes as a surprise-
A sunlight for the soil's eyes.
"The drifts melt and grass grows instead,
And life now blossoms from the dead."

My Old Home

I remember my old home-
White fences against a green mass
Were the meadows of its treasured grass.

I remember my old house-
The tin roof topping the wooden white
And soft rain dancing above at night.

I remember my old tree-
Giant with many arms wanting me to stay
And the sturdy tree house where I used to play.

I remember my old home-
I can see it clearly now but then
It passes gently by me
Like the distant singing wind.

Flowers and Light

Only With You

I want to sail the seven seas,
But only with you.
I want to climb the Rocky Mountains
When I'm with you.

I want to bathe in the Bahamas
With you by my side.
Or watch an Hawaiian sunset
Just us and the sky.

And I want to ski the snowy Alps
If you're there to catch me,
And kiss you in Paris
And in Venice and the South Sea.

I want to travel and fly
With you and only you,
So I'll continue to dream
Until you come true.

Flowers and Light

Kendra Dartez

The Thrill of the Coin

Your love is like finding Spanish gold amidst sand and seaweed.
The thrill of the coin the excitement of discovery
And finding out that something beautiful really could be mine!
But you slipped through my fingers to the ground.
Waves came crashing, erasing what I'd found!
I got to my knees and begged the sea to give you back
But the sea was strong, and the lightning came with a mighty crack!
All I had left was wet sand
All over my knees and upon my hand.
But just because I lost you-
Just like I lost a coin-
I will not curse God
Or drown myself in the sea in quest for you.
I will not waste my time searching by sailing or swimming.
I'll keep my feet on the ground.
I'll keep walking down the beach
Knowing you are now out of reach.
But also knowing there are more mysteries
And surprises to be found along life's way.
Be it pearl, shell, jewelry
Or another surprising discovery!
I'll keep searching along the shore
Looking for you no more
Yet keeping in mind
I'll be more careful next time.
I'll hold on to my treasure tightly.
I'll cling it to my breast
And know I hold the very best!
I'll never let it go.

No storm could take it.
No wave break it.
I'll cherish and keep it close.
So, you are like that coin- old and gone
And I know this now and must move on.
May the sea give you to another
Without reckless fear.
May she hold you ever more dear,
And may I also have love meet me
Somewhere between life's stormy shore and sunlit sea.

Stolen

The tantalizing turn of your head
Made my heart leap like a deer.
And every single word you said
Melted my entire atmosphere.

Just seeing you gave me the day.
I was queen no matter what they'd say.

I was Guinevere, Cleopatra, Josephine, and Juliet;

But like the arduous lovers of old-
The passion died;
My heart stolen so quickly
Was even more quickly sold.

Flowers and Light

Kendra Dartez

Without You

My first love has gone away,
And I can't face another day.
Since he's gone, my heart's been low
But I'll just wait and mend it real slow.

Yet still I must go on my way.
I must see through the long hard day.
What's the use of wanting you?
Cause you don't want me, and we're through.

And, I can walk the miles without you.
I can stand the storms without you.
I won't fall apart and cry,
Cause there's so much I've yet to try.

I can climb the mountains high,
And I can soar through brand new skies.
I can face another day-
With God's help, I'll find my way.

And I can run the race without you.
I can swim through waves without you.
I won't fall apart and cry
Cause there's still life I need to try!

You still must go on your way.
You must see through the long hard day.
Please don't fall apart and cry
Cause there's still life after goodbye!

Flowers and Light

A Petal

I am like a petal upon a rose
About to break away-
A sad, lonely petal that shows
No more color today.

The rosy red of days long past
Dulls from the stained rain.
The whispering wind blew so fast
It beat me and drew pain.

The petal slips ever slowly away
And almost touches fate.
But a loving Hand comes to save,
And brings it to heaven's holy gate.

I am like a spotless white petal
Cleansed and saved today.

Flowers and Light

White Carnation

Other girls want red roses
And large diamond rings,
But I would be just as content
To have a single white carnation-
A symbol of true friendship's adoration.

Roses bloom only in June,
And diamonds are sometimes cast away,
But the lovely little flower
Is innocent, pure and will stay
In bloom for as long as your heart can take.

So, do not rush into love
With roses and diamonds fine,
But wait for the sweet if not as appealing love
Which grows throughout time.

So they can hang their roses
And don their diamond rings,
But my white carnation
Is what true love brings!

Kendra Dartez

I Miss You

I miss you
Like summer misses spring love
And fall yearns for summer's sun.
I miss you
As winter longs for autumn's color
And spring sings to see winter's sky.

I miss you
More as the seasons pass by.
Will summer ever feel spring?
Will fall ever see summer's sun?
Shall winter ever blush?
Shall spring feel winter's touch?
I have seen love birds in summer.
I have seen the sun shine on red and golden leaves.
Somewhere there are palm trees in the winter,
And I've even seen it snow in spring.

I miss you.
But if it is meant to be.
I'll hope, and wait, and see.
See if hope brings yet another time
When seasons break the rhythm,
And true love breaks the rhyme.

Flowers and Light

Kendra Dartez

I Picked It

Along a white picket fence
I saw a red flower all by itself.
I picked it.
Its color was warm and kind,
And I loved it.
I kept it close at all times,
Knowing it might die
And breathed in its pleasant fragrance
With a worried sigh.
The red gave way and gently passed.
So, I lost it.
Petals fell, and there was nothing left,
None like it.
And I passed the white chipped fence
Without it.
Each time I see other bright flowers,
I miss it.
Sometimes I wish I had never
Picked it that day
But I know I'd have it no other way,
For I held love for at least that day!

Flowers and Light

The Water Stirred

When in Rome,
I wished for luck, I wished for love.
Then ancients whispered and the water stirred
And I thought my dream deferred.

In Florence,
I sought Enlightenment.
I prayed in the chapel of Dante.
But not a word was spoken,
And my heart was broken.

In Venice,
My being ached to share the romance
Of the city with another.
I longed for one of the many bridges
To lead me somewhere.
Yet, in that floating city,
I found my voice again.
I sang as if my lover was beside me,
Even though I knew otherwise.
Still, my voice once more followed
The song of my heart.

In Venice, Florence, and Rome,
I found my voice, my faith, my soul!
I had tossed my coins
In the fountain of the unknown.
I wished for luck, I wished to return,
And wished for love pure and true.
The ancients whispered, my heart stirred
And then there was you!

Flowers and Light

Timeless Treasure

You are my timeless treasure.
You are my closest friend.
My knight in shining armor,
You are my everything.

So, I'll cherish my dear treasure.
I'll love my closest friend;
I'll be your beloved maiden
From beginning 'till the end.

And when our timeless treasure
Ages like fine wine,
We'll still be together
Despite the sands of time.

The Pearl

Through both wild storms
And brilliant sunshine,
Our love is like a pearl
Gradually turning
Into something
More beautiful,
Strong,
And fine.

Our Love is Like the Sea

Our love is like the sea-
The waves catching our breath-
Floating on clouds.
The warm sun kissing-
The cool water soothing

Our love is like the sea
In storms or at peace
Whether blue gray or green ocean-
Always powerful and beautiful emotion.

Our love is like the sea.
I with you.
You with me.

Flowers and Light

Our Story

Our book has only just begun
And our story ever new.
Each page is made of love
And tears and laughs all true.

Many chapters have yet to come.
Each word wonderfully anew
And filled and filled with pages,
Pages of me and you.

Our story will continue on
Forever and forever,
Generation to generation,
Love to love,
And on and on.

For our love is evermore old
Page to Page
Age to Age
True Love Forever Told!

Flowers and Light

A Golden Field

Golden wheat frames our backyard softball game.
Everyone who plays knows everyone's name.
Mama's on first and can't catch a thing,
But what smiles and laughter she always seems to bring.
My sister waits on second, ready for the stop
While cousin Andrew plays short-stop.
My brother-n-law is on third; he's always late.
And Daddy waits to catch behind home plate.
My cousin Tim pitches accurate but slow,
And brother John plays right field, always on the go.
Big brother Brian's our center and watches every ball
While I stand in left gazing at them all.
We all wait in the piercing golden sun
As Grandpa steps to bat, wanting a homerun.
He's eighty-nine, but still can swing his bat.
He's slower though, and weaker, but no one tells him that.
The old hazel eyes look the ball over, up, and down.
He makes contact but gives a little frown.
You see he can't round the bases due to his years.
Cousin Jeremy runs them for him…he waits and cheers.
We miss the ball as it rolls along the ground.
Grandpa laughs when he sees Jeremy coming round.
When he touches home plate with easy stride,
Old Grandpa gives him a hug and grins wide.
Even though there's not much time for him to stay,
I know we'll all be together again on a golden field
someday!

Flowers and Light

Legacy of Love

Falling asleep to the sweet sound of your voice
As you read to me.
Feeling your strong, loving arms
Surrounding me
Whenever I skinned a knee.
Looking into the crowd at my games
And knowing you had come to see me.
Watching your proud smile as I crossed the stage
To get my degree.
Praying with you when grandma passed
As we handled grief.
Gazing at your tearful yet joyful eyes
When I was married.
And feeling an overwhelming cycle of love the first time
I held my baby.
For your gift, this legacy of enduring love
You gave to me…
Will never end.
Because now, I too, like you,
Am someone's mommy!

Flowers and Light

My Son

I love you, my son,
From your dancing little toes
To your adorable button nose.
From your square little face
To your hair all out of place.
From your wiry, little thighs
To your twinkling blue eyes.

I love you, my son
From your tiny baby tear
To your grin from ear to ear!
From the first morning's light,
To the endless, sleepless night.

And, I'll love you, my son
From that very first moment's gaze
'Till the end of my days.
You are loved!

Flowers and Light

Daughter of My Heart

Sweet little daughter of my heart
I wait to meet you.
But know I've loved you from the start
Before I even knew…
Before I knew your face, your smile
Before I knew you were you!

For this miracle in my body
Is growing day by day,
And your heart by my heart
Is beating stronger
In wondering, wonderful ways!

With each tiny kick or two
And every moment within…
I wait to meet you.

Will you be a doctor or an athlete?
Or a poet and author too?
Whatever you wish is fine with me…
Just as long as you are you.

For I've loved you from the start
My sweet little daughter…
My brave little woman of my heart.

Flowers and Light

My Summers with You

I'll always remember my summers with you:
Watching thunderstorms from the porch,
Seeing you play your organ at church,
Making the rounds to water the plants,
Sitting outside and watching fireflies dance.

I'll always remember my Christmases at Needwood:
Staring at the soft glow of Christmas tree lights,
Singing Christmas carols in the living room at night,
Listening to your stories of when real sleigh rides took flight.

I'll always remember our trips with you.
Getting knocked down by the waves of the sea,
Sitting in a pink hotel in Ocean City,
Going back with you and visiting your childhood tree.

I'll always remember you, Grandma.
Reading your Bible by the soft lamp light.
Standing firm in your faith and for what's right.
Leading our family toward God's holy light.

So whenever I go to church or play Kippi Koo,
I'll always remember and think fondly of you!

Little Old Tree

Many a year ago
By a country school
In New York,
A little girl of seven or eight
Helped her father
Plant a tree for Arbor Day.
When they finished,
A gleam of humble pride
Shone in her small, bright eyes.

Sixty seven years then passed,
And the little girl had grown up fast.
I, her granddaughter, and my family
Traveled back
To the same small town
Where she had grown up.

We saw her small house
And then rode on past
Until the petite,
Grey-haired lady said, "Stop!"
We stopped and all piled out.
"Little Old Tree!" my Grandma said
As she marched along
Toward the tree dead ahead.
"Little Old Tree," she whispered again.

And I looked at that tree
Where my dear grandmother stood,

And saw not a little old tree
But instead, a tall sturdy wood!
Then I smiled as I saw
A gleam of glowing pride
Had appeared in my Grandma's old eyes.

Kendra Dartez

Out of the Shadows

The silver moon glowed through the dark forest,
Lighting his path.
The tree's angry shadows attacked him,
Causing great wrath.

He raced through the wicked timber,
Seeking his pack.
He sniffed for friend or foe,
Staying on track.

Thunder clouds sprang into the dark sky,
Bringing the rain.
It soaked down to the bone,
Causing chilled pain.

On through the storm he whimpered,
Trying to fight.
On through the lonesome darkness,
Moonlight in sight.

The rain stopped and the sky cleared,
Bringing the full moon.
He raced from out of the shadows,
He'd be there soon.

He walked slowly to the cliff's edge,
Overlooking the night.
He gazed at the silver moon,
Shining there bright.

He cried to the moon and to the sky,
Challenging the forest.

And as he howled, voices joined him-
 Singing in chorus.

He opened his mouth to sing again,
 Howling full to the sky.
And by the full moon the pack came,
 Upon hearing the wolf's cry.

Sailing in the Sky

I see your boat still sailing,
Sailing in the sky.
So for now, sweet father,
For now we say goodbye.

And though our hearts are broken
And could not miss you more,
We know one day you'll greet us
On that brightly shining shore.

The Lark

Ruth left yesterday
Like a rose thirsty for water.

She was the best teacher, mother, grandmother,
Counselor, and friend.

Ruth, with her fiery star eyes
Moved on like a wounded lark rising
Ever so gently.
Rising and singing
Above the dusty, dark clouds.

And after Ruth left,
My heart simply wept.

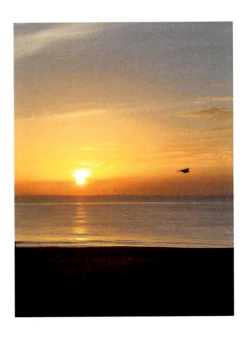

In God We Trust

Thousands of voices
Ashen faces, crumbled lives,
We will remember you.
We have heard your cry.
We have watched your pain
And shall promise
This will not happen again.
Lord, grant us the wisdom
In the midst of the storm.
Turn our eyes from tragedy to eternity.
From despair to hope.
From evil to goodness.
From death to life.
Take mercy on us.
Heal us; strengthen us.
Guide us; deliver us.
Let your mighty hand
Keep us from the enemy.
Shine on our Land again
And let freedom never end!

Flowers and Light

Autumn Has Come

Autumn has come to my years,
But there is no need for tears.
For what might have been
Has turned its color up on end.
Orange, yellow, red
Leaves flutter boldly by
As if to say
Fear not
Though summer waves its goodbye!
A new season vibrantly says
Fall in love with me instead.
There are more ways
To catch the eye
As each year goes by.
Autumn has come to my years.
The changing colors
Replacing green with gold
And turning crisp, new,
And unapologetically bold!

Flowers and Light

Dare to Discover

Dare to discover the person inside.
Know how to laugh and know how to cry.
Dare to discover a newfound friend.
Share when you laugh and share when you cry.
Dare to discover a person in need.
Help them to laugh and no longer to cry.
Dare to always wonder about the world.
Find the wonder of you and the wonder of why.
Dare to discover throughout your life.
It is a dare to never let your dreams subside.
A dare to laugh.
A dare to cry.
A dare to dream.
A dare to fly!

Flowers and Light

A Time to Sing

You gave my heart a time to sing,
Then stole my love, my everything.
I opened up my love to you;
It only lasted one day through
Like the blushing hibiscus flowers,
Love only bloomed a few, short hours.

So my heart tries to beat a new song,
But it wonders what went wrong.
I cling to God to make it right,
And He says wait, everything is right.

For He can make the ocean drum,
Make wheat fields dance and beehives hum.
He can make the willows whisper and eagles cry.
Make fireflies glow and winter wind sigh.
He knows the sparrow's song from beginning to end;
So, somehow, I too, will learn to sing again.

Flowers and Light

Kendra Dartez

ABOUT THE AUTHOR

Kendra Dartez has a B.S. in English and an M.S. in Education. She worked as a school librarian for a few years and now works as a children's programmer at her local public library. She enjoys reading, writing, singing, traveling, taking pictures, playing pretend with her kids, and playing sports with her family. She lives with her husband, two children, and several books in rural Virginia.

Made in the USA
San Bernardino, CA
12 February 2018